Proverbs for Christian Living

Other books by Dr. Monroe Gaultney

Spiritual Snacks: A Devotional Bible Study

Eating the Scroll: Bible Study for Small Groups

God's Menu: A Life Application Bible Study

Recipes for Hungry Christians

PROVERBS

FOR

CHRISTIAN LIVING

By Dr. Monroe Gaultney

Resource *Publications*

An imprint of *Wipf and Stock Publishers*
199 West 8th Avenue • Eugene OR 97401

PROVERBS FOR CHRISTIAN LIVING

Resource Publications
A division of Wipf and Stock Publishers
199 W 8th Ave, Suite 3
Eugene, OR 97401

Proverbs for Christian Living
By Gaultney, Monroe

ISBN: 1-59752-170-1
Publication date 5/5/2005

DEDICATION

Proverbs for Christian Living is dedicated to four very wise and caring people who have been a blessing to everyone who has ever known them. Lela Farmer, Frances Farmer, Joe Johnson and Jane Johnson, because of those whose lives you have touched, your firm beliefs and loving wisdom will continue to encourage countless others who may never even know your name.

CONTENTS

FOREWORD

In *Proverbs for Christian Living,* Monroe Gaultney exhibits a fresh brain-teasing approach to teaching scriptural truth. These catchy proverbs will flash across America and around the world on church signs, illuminating the darkness reflected in this lost world with hope and inspiration.

Dr.Eddie G. Grigg, President
New Life Theological Seminary

PREFACE

These proverbs and sayings were written after reading the epistle of First John. I pray that they will prove to be useful and meaningful in some way.

The same literary styles that shaped the Biblical proverbs as well as the parables of Jesus provided the framework for each proverb and maxim in this book.

For those wondering why anyone should still try to teach the gospel in this way, the answer is simple: **Because Jesus did.** The proverbs are in random order in each chapter. If topics repeat themselves in other verses, additional proverbs address the subject. Both proverbs and chapters are numbered for ease of reference.

Blessings,
Monroe Gaultney, 2005

CHAPTER 1

TAKE IT FROM THE BEGINNING

> That which was from the beginning, which we have heard, which we have seen with our eyes, which we have looked at and our hands have touched—this we proclaim concerning the Word of life. The life appeared; we have seen it and testify to it, and we proclaim to you the eternal life, which was with the Father and has appeared to us. **1 John 1:1–2 NIV**

1) I reached for God's hand, and He gave me His heart.
2) I knocked on God's door and Jesus let me in.
3) The compassionate introduce God to their friends.
4) Jesus crossed the line that separated us from God.
5) Explain God's forgiveness plainly.
6) To know God is to love Him, and to love God is to love others.
7) Life with Christ is a choice: Choose Christ for life.
8) Read Christ's biography and meet the Man.
9) God and Christ are only two sides of the triangle.

10) Jesus' story includes all of us.

11) It has been said that Christ has always been with God, but can that be said of you?

12) Forcing God upon the unwilling is like pushing a tree up their nose.

13) Salvation needs no financing; Jesus paid it all.

14) Be a proclaiming explainer, not a profaning complainer.

15) These riddles I fling into the air: Is "God" His name or His nature? Is "Heavenly Father" who God is, or merely His title? When we call upon the Lord God, who will answer, Father or Son?

16) Happiness is sharing Jesus, because God shared Him with us.

17) Encounter God by talking with Jesus; experience God by trusting in Christ.

18) We tell what we know because of Whom we know, and we know Him because we know Christ.

19) When we tell His-story, history repeats itself.

20) To stroll with Christ is to walk with God.

Dear Lord, grant me the confidence and boldness to share my personal experiences and knowledge of you with others. Amen.

CHAPTER 2

JOY AND FELLOWSHIP

> We proclaim to you what we have seen and heard, so that you also may have fellowship with us. And our fellowship is with the Father and with his Son, Jesus Christ. We write this to make our joy complete. **1 John 1:3–4 NIV**

1) The wise meet together in God's house, but the haughty have forgotten His address.
2) The cross is a good place to start a friendship.
3) Accept God's forgiveness and forgive each other.
4) Kneeling with others can be an uplifting experience.
5) A walk with Christ may not always be a stroll in the garden, but it will never be a walk alone.
6) If you are so happy in Christ, then why are you grumpy to me?
7) God is there for those who are there for others.
8) As we strengthen others, God strengthens us.
9) The old story will always be new to someone.
10) Like a mother's unceasing love for her wayward child is a Christian's love for a wayward friend.
11) Leading others to closeness with God begins with Jesus before breakfast.

12) Like a fire in a parched field, our joy grows when others respond to Him.

13) It is easier to sing praises in a choir than to harmonize alone.

14) The gospel you heard is still good to hear, so tell it.

15) Those who visit with God in the morning are blessed all day long.

16) To experience Christ is to enjoy fellowship with the Father; and fellowship with the Father comes through closeness to Christ.

Dear Lord, increase my joy in fellowship with others, and increase their joy in me. Amen.

CHAPTER 3
WITHOUT SHADOWS

> This is the message we have heard from him and declare to you: God is light; in him there is no darkness at all. **1 John 1:5 NIV**

1) Like ants running from a stomping shoe, darkness gives way to God.
2) Those keeping Christ to themselves hold Him at a distance.
3) God is not a God of shadows.
4) Shadows disappear when the Son is directly overhead.
5) God's light shines from the inside out, but darkness seeks to block it out.
6) Holding up the Christ of the cross lights the way for others.
7) Darkness runs from light and hides from God.
8) Jesus is pure, death is sure, and life without God is no life at all.
9) As shadows run from light, truth basks in the warmth of His love.
10) Look on the bright side: Look up.

11) Who has trouble seeing His light? Those who keep "Son" glasses on remain in the dark.

12) We heard. We believed. We live.

13) Those to whom Christ has made a difference, make a difference in the world.

Dear Lord, may I always see your light, and pass it on to others. Amen.

CHAPTER 4

A LIGHT STROLL

> If we claim to have fellowship with him yet walk in the darkness, we lie and do not live by the truth. But if we walk in the light, as he is in the light, we have fellowship with one another, and the blood of Jesus, his Son, purifies us from all sin. **1 John 1:6–7 NIV**

1) God's faithfulness fuels Christian fellowship.
2) Seeds of dissention struggle to grow in the light of Christ.
3) A stopwatch can't measure God's forgiving nature.
4) Father and Son: Forgiveness, Incorporated.
5) God's soul-cleaning business uses Jesus Soap.
6) Confession signs an agreement with God.
7) Experiencing God is more than experiencing good.
8) God's light opens understanding's door so the fallen can dart quickly in.
9) Liars lie, but lovers love.
10) A sinful life harbors dark memories, but a godly life is not forgotten.

11) Dark nights chase sunlight, but God's love knows no darkness.

12) False light slowly turns into darkness, but God's word sheds eternal light.

13) The wise stroll with God in the cool of the day, but fools search for water in the desert at noon.

14) The wise work for God; but God is self-employed.

15) It is good to be good, but it is better to walk with God.

16) Sliding back into sin's mud hole leaves God on high ground.

17) God minds His business; be mindful of God.

18) Beware of the hungry dark; it yearns to swallow Christians whose lights flicker and sputter.

19) Unlimited hugs are wrapped and ready in the heart of true believers.

20) False believers offer false hope.

21) Those who call God a liar overload their mouth.

Dear Lord, I choose life. I choose light. I choose you. Guide me as we walk through this thing called life together. Amen.

CHAPTER 5

NO SIN? NO WAY!

> But if we walk in the light, as he is in the light, we have fellowship with one another, and the blood of Jesus, his Son, purifies us from all sin. If we claim to be without sin, we deceive ourselves and the truth is not in us. **1 John 1:7–8 NIV**

1) Some say sin is OK, but sin's bullet awaits all at the OK Morale.
2) When we believe our own lies, our lies become our beliefs.
3) Change your sinning obsession to winning confession.
4) We are born to be born again.
5) We were born in sin to sin, and we need no training.
6) Self-deceit promises a pleasant present, but delivers a tainted tomorrow.
7) Liars sin and sinners lie; but sins confessed are sins that die.
8) Sin drives a wedge between our humanity and God's divinity, but Christ chauffeurs the wedge back home.
9) Christ gives us power to change our nature, but our sinful nature hates change.

10) Those whose sins are forgiven are looking to Christ, but those who sin without looking are looking the wrong way.

11) For fools, Christ's forgiveness is a crutch to help them live with themselves; but for the wise His forgiveness is a step toward living with God.

12) When we say we don't need Christ, we aren't Christians, we're liars.

13) It is easier to store ice in a furnace than to walk with God while denying our sin.

14) When we choose to run with God, Christ sets the pace.

15) Appeal for God's forgiveness decreases as denial increases.

16) Those who declare no need for God have acclimated to emptiness.

17) Sins denied are sins we choose to keep.

18) We lose sin when we choose God.

19) Sin: Self-Inflicted Nails.

20) Sin: Self-Indulgence Now.

21) When we dare to walk with God, only Christ can keep us in step.

22) Are we sinners because we sin, or do we sin because we are sinners?

23) Denial destroys our vision of God, and distorts our view of ourselves.

Dear Lord, sometimes I fail to listen during my own confession, and at other times I lie to you because I have denied the truth about myself. Make me more sensitive and responsive to the truth. Amen.

CHAPTER 6

NO CONFLICT OF INTEREST

> If we confess our sins, he is faithful and just and will forgive us our sins and purify us from all unrighteousness. If we claim we have not sinned, we make him out to be a liar and his word has no place in our lives. **1 John 1:9–10 NIV**

1) Daredevils who defy God lose the dare.
2) Peer forgiveness is fine, but God's forgiveness is divine.
3) God will always be true to His nature.
4) We are God's goods and Christ is minding the store.
5) God's nature knows no mood swings and He never quarrels with Himself.
6) God's guarantee can be trusted and His services are always within praying distance.
7) Man's spirit rises and falls like the river tide, but God's faithfulness keeps our ship afloat.
8) Those who fight sin without God's help challenge the rapids alone; but the waterfall awaits.
9) The fool laughs at the need for forgiveness, but God weeps at the fool's folly.

10) The forgiven agree with God about their sin, but deniers spit upon His Son.

11) The wise accept God's grace for the small price of a prayer, but fools will cry bitter tears for the fleeting joy of sin.

12) Sin flows from a polluted river, but forgiveness cascades from God's grace.

13) Only after the proud fall do they admit their need for God.

14) We can't walk with God when our back is to the Son.

15) Those denying their sins are refusing the healing salve of God's forgiveness.

16) It is better to be chained to a comet than to fight with God.

17) God's forgiveness is available upon request.

18) Those who walk with God walk with confidence.

19) Seeing what God can make us, makes us look at who we've become.

20) Christ in you will not lie to the Father, and God's spirit will not lie to you.

21) Confession comes from a broken heart; God's forgiveness heals the hurt.

22) Even delayed confession and repentance reaches the compassionate ears of the Most High.

Dear Lord, I know I sin. Keep me alert enough to know when I sin and to admit it to you immediately. Amen.

Chapter 7

HAVE YOU USED YOUR SIN-BLOCK TODAY?

> My dear children, I write this to you so that you will not sin. But if anybody does sin, we have one who speaks to the Father in our defense—Jesus Christ, the Righteous One. He is the atoning sacrifice for our sins, and not only for ours but also for the sins of the whole world. **1 John 2:1–2 NIV**

1) God never feels good about sin, and sin never feels good about God.
2) Our bath is drawn, and His righteousness is ready to scour our sins with loving hands.
3) Sin doesn't just happen; it's orchestrated.
4) God created the CROSS road for sinners.
5) Dare to pray for sin-resisting power, and you will no longer be irresistible to sin.
6) Emptying beer bottles until we are full will not be fulfilling for long.
7) Sin's temptations are invitations to exploitation and depravation.
8) Sin has our name tattooed on its strongest arm.
9) The CROSS road leads to God's forgiveness.
10) Dare not enter God's court without Christ.

11) Meditate and contemplate the value of your mediator.

12) The harms of sin and germs would take forever to count.

13) Sin knows our name, and says it often.

14) Confession and repentance puts new shoes on our feet.

15) We sometimes block light from the sun, but the Son blocks our sin from God.

16) Sin feels good for a season, but seasons change.

17) It is impossible for the impure to contact the holiness of God, but Jesus makes the impossible *possible*.

18) The only guard against sin is commitment to God; but sin leans against the guardrail and pushes with all its might.

19) It is not true that sin's clutches can never be pried loose; but it is true that the tenacity of sin is no match for the power of God.

20) God is faithful even when we are faithless.

21) Those who decide in advance not to sin spend less time among the rocks.

22) It is safer to spit in the face of an angry bear than to think God is lying about sin.

23) Is sin sniffing at your door? Lock the door and give Jesus the key.

24) To prepare your life, read the manufacturer's label.

25) The chances we will sin are more predictable than the shouts of an angry man.

26) Like mighty oak trees, let our hearts reach for the Son.

27) The deadly snake curls comfortably around the feet of those who deny their sin.

28) Like lava blanketing rocky ground, God's forgiveness covers our sin.

29) Jesus stands ready to steady the ladder, so the shaken and forsaken can climb out of the pit.

30) Who will be your defense counsel when you stand before the Judge?

31) Dodge sin; spend time with Jesus.

32) God minds His own business; be mindful of God.

33) We wrong God by doing wrong.

34) Deny sin; deny God.

35) Time spent with Jesus gives negativity little time to grow.

36) Threads may still unravel, but the quilt will not be lost.

37) Before the rope was looped around the cleat, its purpose was already decided.

38) The ship's course is charted and set before the sail kisses the sky.

39) Jesus stands up for His disciples, though they fall again and again; and though they stumble time after time, He lifts them up and sends them out again.

40) If sin makes us feel bad, that is good; but when sin makes us feel good, that is bad.

41) It is easier to continue in wrongdoing than to do what is right.

42) It is not right to think that wrong and its relatives have relative values; God's values remain absolute every day.

43) There is only one way into the eye of a needle, and there is only one way out

44) Sin's din has a thousand doors.

45) Without Jesus to intercede on our behalf, we don't stand half a chance.

46) Two things the Lord has revealed to me; even three certainties I have come to know: The humble kneel in His presence, but the proud are bent by woe; the wise stand in His strength, but the fool falls from weakness; the righteous soar with angels; but the ungodly dive with demons.

Jesus, I know that I sin, but I am truly bothered by it. Thanks for being there for me. I desire deeply to be as faithful to you as you are to me. Amen.

CHAPTER 8

LOVE, REVERENCE, AND OBEDIENCE

> We know that we have come to know him if we obey his commands. The man who says, "I know him," but does not do what he commands is a liar, and the truth is not in him. **1 John 2:3–4 NIV**

1) True love is never dormant.
2) Those who believe in Christ want to do what He did.
3) Like trees with empty branches in winter, it is easy to believe there is no spring.
4) Apathy and denial are debits in God's books.
5) Beware of those who keep their own commandments, and shun the fools who make up their own rules.
6) The wise follow the Master's teachings, and their hands and feet confirm their commitment.
7) The self-proclaimed follow the Christ of convenience, but the righteous follow the Christ of the Cross.
8) Fools cast their lot with the people's choice, but though their vote be cast, it will not be counted.

9) The religious know God's decrees, but the righteous obey His Word.

10) Puny plants in well-tended ground may grow strong and tall; but sterling seed left unattended may not grow at all.

11) Many claim to know God even when God doesn't know them.

12) Christ's teachings are God's teachings; but blended faith portrays a false future.

13) As the mouse hides from the hawk, the hypocrite dodges righteousness.

14) It is easier to chew a roasted snowball than to please God without obedience.

15) Plastic fruit doesn't grow in God's orchards; nor are silk flowers found in his bouquet.

16) Who are not faithful to the teaching of the Lord? Those whose tears don't wash His feet.

17) Who are those who love God? Those who love Christ and stand on His word.

18) It is better to spend one day with Jesus than to spend a lifetime with wealth.

19) When commitment leads, obedience follows.

20) Submit to God's will as Christ did, even when the short-term outcome promises pain.

21) When you name the fruit, you name the tree.

22) His followers know who they are, because they know who He is.

23) When grapes despise the vine, their juice sours before the harvest.

24) The right path challenges the faith of many, and enduring faith keeps them on the right path.

Dear Lord, I don't want to live a lie. Overfill me with your love, and bless me with commitment for obedience. Amen.

CHAPTER 9

PERFECT LOVE

> But if anyone obeys his word, God's love is truly made complete in him. This is how we know we are in him: Whoever claims to live in him must walk as Jesus did. **1 John 2:5–6 NIV**

1) God's tailor uses a cross for his measure.
2) She who speaks His word reaches for His hand.
3) God's love jumps from the pages of His Book.
4) When we are mistaken for Jesus, we are who God wants us to be; and when we are thought to be His twin, Jesus smiles.
5) God perfects His love in us as we meet His expectations; and He expects us to follow Jesus all our days.
6) It is better to live His word than to memorize it; and it is better to give His love than to seek it.
7) Our walk weaves and our talk deceives when His Word doesn't leap from our lips.
8) His righteousness reveals the fakers and puts the wayward in the news.
9) Oh, that my love would be less shallow, and that my life would cast His shadow.

10) God's love lives in a house built by His word; and that house is constantly adding rooms.

11) His love is given freely but perfected in few.

12) The disciplined may give out, but they never give up.

13) Only those close to Jesus are under His shadow.

14) When His way becomes our way, we will be His all the way.

15) Before one can do what Jesus would do in one's own situation, one must be willing to do what He did in His.

16) While surface believers lie panting on the ground, true disciples gain strength in a boiling pot.

17) As His Word becomes our word, His love becomes our love.

18) When perfectionism turns toward God, righteousness locks it in a vault and hides the key.

19) The righteous keep their word about keeping His Word.

20) Words that conflict with His Word contradict His life.

21) Eyes that look up to Him will look out for others.

22) Those whose feet follow His feet spend much time on their knees.

23) God's love holds true even when ours collapses in on itself.

24) As His sandaled feet pressed into the sand, His love left an everlasting impression.

25) Those who step in His footprints enjoy the pleasure of His presence.

26) Whose mouth will not utter the promise of God? Whose feet will stray from God's path? All whose way isn't under His light; and those making promises they will not keep.

27) As we live His word, His word gives us life.

Dear Lord, I pray that I will live a life that makes you proud to present me to our Heavenly Father. Amen.

CHAPTER 10

NOTHING NEW

> Dear friends, I am not writing you a new command but an old one, which you have had since the beginning. This old command is the message you have heard. Yet I am writing you a new command; its truth is seen in him and you, because the darkness is passing and the true light is already shining. **1 John 2:7–8 NIV**

1) The astute salute absolute truth.
2) God's light makes darkness cower in the corner.
3) Love one another with the compassion of Christ, and the Lord's compassion will grow within you.
4) Love your neighbor as if he lives in your mirror.
5) God's grace arrives first, and His forgiveness skids in right behind it.
6) God's message is not new, but the ears of the universe still long to hear it.
7) Selfish ambition and pride poison the congregation's well.
8) Like a giant redwood among a forest of red cedars, His truth stunts the stature of seemingly significant sayings.
9) It is better to illuminate one truth from His Word than to accept a thousand dark pearls of gray wisdom.

10) A perilous rut of confusion awaits all who foolishly kick the ends off God's ~~t~~**rut** ~~h~~.

11) God's truth is a universe of love, but the world's truth is a den of doubt.

12) Philosophers whiz past obvious truth, vainly in search of themselves.

13) His conclusion diffuses confusion for all who follow Christ.

14) The Word that begins life is the Word that began life.

15) The darkness in the night of our soul can't hide from God's eternal lantern.

16) When God's truth is our truth, truth will truly be ours.

17) Neither maliciousness nor abiding anger is welcoming to our Lord.

18) Christ's teachings can be new to the old who meet Him late in life, and old for the young who met Him early.

19) Like a wounded animal hiding in the dark, darkness retreats from His revealing light.

20) Like a deer fleeing from a hound, run from teachings not grounded in Christ.

21) Love your neighbor as yourself; love both yourself and your neighbor.

22) In which word should we abide? Who alone speaks words that impart wisdom and love? God's Words are more solid than stone; His living Word gives life.

Dear Lord, help me to love my neighbor as myself. Amen.

CHAPTER 11

OUT OF DARKNESS

> Anyone who claims to be in the light but hates his brother is still in the darkness. Whoever loves his brother lives in the light, and there is nothing in him to make him stumble. But whoever hates his brother is in the darkness and walks around in the darkness; he does not know where he is going, because the darkness has blinded him. **1 John 2:9–11 NIV**

1) Darkness eats souls.
2) Don't play in the dark unless you plan to stay.
3) Creditable Christians create love letters with their lives.
4) Stumbling believers lack God's light.
5) Look not upon God's family with darkness in your heart.
6) Darkness guns for light because it loves to fight.
7) Hate wears a cloud of portable darkness; and stumbling mars its walk.
8) God's love doesn't dine with hate, and darkness won't share a room with light.
9) God's love nourishes; God's Spirit enlightens.
10) Learn to love the unlovable and downtrodden.

11) God's love is our light; and His mighty torch lights our way.
12) Lead a life of spite, and die a dark death.
13) Love is binding, but hate is blinding.
14) Hate generates hate, but love fosters love.
15) Even the fool chooses love over hate; but for the righteous, hate is not ever a choice.
16) His love heals hate.
17) Love and hate aren't roommates.
18) The fool is at home in a house of hatred.
19) Some love to hate, and others hate to love, but those who love to love make all the difference.
20) Christians who hate Christians love neither God nor man.
21) God's children worship together, whether the weather is good or bad.
22) Can a Christian really hate another Christian? Can Christ actually hate Himself?
23) It is better to live a day in God's love than to have power over the whole world.
24) Love your brothers and sisters in the Lord because the Lord loves your brothers and sisters.
25) Hate is not God's child; hate is born in hell.
26) Love doesn't come from hate, and hate doesn't come from love.
27) Leave the life of lust for power; learn the power of love.

Dear Lord, I give you my hate and accept your love. Amen.

CHAPTER 12

FORGIVENESS IS GOD'S TO GIVE

I write to you, dear children, because your sins have been forgiven on account of his name. **1 John 2:12 NIV**

1) Jesus is not a thief who steals sin. We must give it to Him.
2) Stop treating sinfulness as if it is all you deserve.
3) Sin is the currency used to buy our souls.
4) Give up your sins and be forgiven.
5) Our darkest moments and heaviest sins are light loads for God.
6) The forgiven release their grip on sin and God sets their souls free.
7) God has more forgiveness than we have sins, and we have more sins than we have sense.
8) Repentant prisoners admit their crimes to Jesus, and God grants them full pardons.
9) Feel free to hold on to sin until it kills you, because it will.
10) Like a porcupine kissing a balloon, God's touch destroys sin.

11) God's forgiveness comes with a life-back guarantee, but the fool waits for something more.

12) Forgiveness is ours upon request; but worldly wisdom doubts the simplicity of the system.

13) God's forgiveness is given with a smile, but the doubter feels the warmth of neither.

14) The bill for sin always comes due.

15) Forgiveness removes spots from our soul, but the weak long for the familiar stains.

16) Jesus forgives what we give Him, but sins we hoard hobble our spirit.

17) Shame prefers to drown in sin, but repentance welcomes the rescuer.

18) Jesus gave and God forgives, but skeptics deny the evidence.

19) Whether to drown in sin-born sorrows or to swim in the eternal spring of forgiveness is a choice few think they have.

20) As quickly as God forgives their sins, fools want them back.

21) It is better that God sweep sin from under your skin than to be surrounded by a thousand friends.

22) Sin is for sale, not for short-term lease.

23) Even though Christ knows your type, he still gave blood for you.

24) Dangling freely from Christ's outstretched hands are the keys of forgiveness.

25) Send your sins to God with no return address.

26) The Son delivered God's letter of forgiveness to us all.

27) The price of sin is higher than anyone can afford to pay.

Dear Lord, please forgive me for all the times I haven't asked for forgiveness. Amen.

CHAPTER 13

DO YOU KNOW?

> I write to you, fathers, because you have known Him who is from the beginning. I write to you, young men, because you have overcome the evil one. I write to you, dear children, because you have known the Father. I write to you, fathers, because you have known Him who is from the beginning. I write to you, young men, because you are strong, and the word of God lives in you, and you have overcome the evil one. **1 John 2:13–14 NIV**

1) When prayer becomes an afterthought, sin needs no forethought.
2) A diary of answered prayers keeps the memory strong.
3) Let the taste of victory over sin make you thirst for more.
4) God invited me to come and talk, but like a fool, I didn't show up.
5) Water is wet, deserts are dry, and God's loving grace is eternal.
6) Remember God all of your days, and fly on the wings of faith.
7) Scavengers and bottom-feeders don't swim with Jesus.

8) So many call upon God in drought, but forget his name when the well is full.

9) Those who forget Christ fall into the bottomless canyon of despair.

10) Walking on water was a wondrous thing; and walking with Jesus puts us on top.

11) Remember your wins, and let your defeats be your instructor.

12) The righteous know God personally, but the religious only know God's rules.

13) We may not see God perform, but He always signs His work.

14) That God is here, few deny; but that He can be known, few try.

15) Keep a diary of God's love and faithfulness so that you may be reassured in uncertain days.

16) Living without God is as easy as putting a saddle upon a sparrow.

17) It is easier to forget God's intervention than to forget our troubles.

18) The simple are content just to know who God is; but for the righteous spiritual growth is a way of life.

19) Knowing who God is shouts who we're not.

20) Once I saw what God can do, my own limitations shouted their name.

21) Fools sabotage their relationship with God by forgetting the victories He gave them.

22) Remember God's faithfulness all of your days, and His power will lead the way.

23) A short memory is denial's prisoner.

24) If you met Christ once, then He is still around.

25) The evil one's show of strength is but a puppet show to God.

26) God's open-door policy is a policy of power.

Dear Lord, I want to draw as close to you as you are to me. Amen.

CHAPTER 14
WORLDLY LOVE

> Do not love the world or anything in the world. If anyone loves the world, the love of the Father is not in him. For everything in the world—the cravings of sinful man, the lust of his eyes and the boasting of what he has and does—comes not from the Father but from the world. The world and its desires pass away, but the man who does the will of God lives forever. **1 John 2:15–17 NIV**

1) The Heavenly Father does not negotiate with sin.
2) Allow God's love to seal your love inside His.
3) The Father's love and worldly love begin their march back to back.
4) God's love is ignored by many, but worldly love is embraced by most.
5) Loving the world's goods means hating the Father's goodness.
6) Love God with all you are, and love the person you become.
7) Shun worldliness, desire holiness, and forget what might have been.
8) Those who worship the world's wisdom waste their mind.

9) Power addicts and pleasure slaves make their souls the devil's gift.

10) Sin is a cancerous monster with sharp teeth and bulldog jaws.

11) The godly shun the world's stunning ways, but the greedy choose and lose.

12) Friendship with the world is hatred toward God, but God's love evicts desires that maim.

13) God's love rebuilds houses ripped apart by the winds of sin; but too many remain in the condemned house they know.

14) The self-righteous shout their spirituality, but the righteous enjoy quiet time with God.

15) God's love is pure and His ways strange to a world that demands a logical path.

16) The impatient force reason upon the world, but the patient wait upon the Lord.

17) The unwary are wooed by the world's charms, but the faithful know that the price is too high.

18) The young love the excitement of war, but the wise prefer the thrill of God's love.

19) The uncommitted straddle the fence between God and sin, but the righteous stay off the fence and in the yard.

20) One can't love worldly things with God's love; because God's love isn't attracted to sin.

21) Like fire during a drought, lust destroys the strongest of trees.

22) Who can climb that holy hill? Those who allow God's love to pull them there.

23) Bragging neither springs from God's fountain, nor blooms in heaven's trees.

24) One walks with head held high only after bowing it low.

25) Boasting may boost the ego, but it kills the reputation.

26) The world's way isn't the way up.

27) Those driven by self-loathing deny God's goodness.

28) God doesn't claim all who claim to know Him.

29) If worldly pleasure is what you're here after, then the hereafter holds no pleasure for you.

30) Those refusing the love of God are rejecting the God of love.

Dear Lord, worldly things attract me. I pray for good judgment in how I spend my time, thoughts, and energy. I want to exchange the ups and downs of worldly desires for your steady, long-term love.

CHAPTER 15

ARE THE ANTICHRISTS CHURCH BABIES?

> Dear children, this is the last hour; and as you have heard that the antichrist is coming, even now many antichrists have come. This is how we know it is the last hour. They went out from us, but they did not really belong to us. For if they had belonged to us, they would have remained with us; but their going showed that none of them belonged to us. **1 John 2:18–19 NIV**

1) The hands of the clock will appear broken in the final hour.
2) These last days may be long, but twilight settles quietly over the land.
3) Beware of those who create three religions out of two and blend the third with a fourth.
4) God's churches aren't founded on petty arguments.
5) In the final days, the straight and narrow will be sold as a twisted and convoluted hardship; and the broad road will be adorned with fools-gold and costume jewelry.
6) Antichrists sell their truth with the solemnity of a mortician.

7) Antichrists deliver doubt to Christians' beliefs, but those solidly rooted in Christ will not be moved.

8) Many look for the devil in the street, but few expect him in a pew.

9) Like the hunted that fears the hunter, flee from an altered gospel.

10) Our final hour for ministry is the one we're in.

11) Religion-blenders are contenders against the cross.

12) Congregation raiders are enemies of the church.

13) Beware of panthers pretending to be kittens all cuddled up in their pew.

14) Those hostile to the fundamentals of faith have never crawled to the Cross of Christ.

15) Haughty spirits are spirits not yet broken.

16) Though the words of the contentious be sweet, their words burn like bubbling tar.

17) Though the antichrist's feet appear to be planted on the Word, they are really roots reaching up from hell.

18) The last days may last for a while, so be prepared to last.

19) May challengers of your faith lose the challenge before you meet.

20) Change the hard Gospel into a soft-sell; hammer another nail through His hands.

21) Beware of those who are quick to teach God's teachings, but slow to introduce the teacher.

22) It is better to sleep with vipers than to lead God's children astray.

23) In the final days, amazing grace will be thought a maze; and lessons on grace will be used to confuse those who search for God.

24) It is easier to listen to streams of logic than to hear testimonies of faith.

25) Those who leapfrog from church to church make many friends on the shallow side of the pond.

26) Disharmony within creates hostility without.

27) Those not knowing who Jesus is know no one of importance.

28) Be wary of professional Christians; they profit from their faith at the expense of others.

29) Those who aren't for Him are against Him by default, whether it is their fault or not.

30) Ministers of Christ leave believers with answers, while skeptics tease an admiring herd with their questions.

31) All church members may not be Christians, and all Christians may not be church members, but true believers remain true.

Dear Lord, help me to recognize the antichrists for what they are, and to keep separate from them. Amen.

CHAPTER 16
ANOINTED

> But you have an anointing from the Holy One, and all of you know the truth. I do not write to you because you do not know the truth, but because you do know it and because no lie comes from the truth. **I John 2:20–21 NIV**

1) Christ is the first page of God's book.
2) Separating truth from lies is not the liar's job.
3) Let the fire of God's Word set your heart ablaze once a day, all day long.
4) Lies devour the truth, and gossip spreads like ink spilled upon a rug.
5) God's truth won't piggy-back with deceit, and false piety shrinks from His presence.
6) Desire God's anointing above all knowledge.
7) The blameless have an anointing of truth, and the righteous are not deceived.
8) God appoints and the Holy Spirit anoints.
9) God anoints the righteous with truth, but scoffers pick their own brain.
10) God's truth is the blueprint of the faithful, but the faithless are their own architects.
11) Those guided by God point to what is right; but the deluded introduce a swan's reflection as its twin.

12) The Bible is the answer book for God's anointed; but the self-appointed question the answers without answering the questions.

13) The righteous won't stray from His way, but doubters have neither compass nor map.

14) God's truth inspires visions of hope, but Satan's lies are laden with empty dreams.

15) The anointed walk toward Christ Jesus while praising God, but cynics waltz in circles while praising the band.

16) Miners of His Word move higher by digging deeper.

17) God pours His truth into the heads of those whose hearts are His.

18) God gives discernment to those concerned about truth.

19) When God's truth pierces the veil of sin, understanding floods the soul.

20) When God's Spirit touches the believer, false religion is thrown out by its ear.

21) They who know God know truth.

22) The spider of sin weaves webs of woe within shades and shadows of doubt.

23) True believers are loyal to His way, but pretenders pay homage to change.

24) Like a gamecock bred to fight, the godless attack His Word for sport.

25) The sin-spinner from hell is not a beginner as well.

Dear Lord, anoint me with your Holy Spirit that I may know the truth. Amen.

CHAPTER 17
LIARS AND DENIERS

> Who is the liar? It is the man who denies that Jesus is the Christ. Such a man is the anti-christ—he denies the Father and the Son. No one who denies the Son has the Father; whoever acknowledges the Son has the Father also. **1 John 2:22–23 NIV**

1) For liars and tryers, "almost" is enough.
2) Deniers lie, and liars deny.
3) The storm rages, the midday sun burns hot upon the fields, and God scorns all who scoff at His Son.
4) Repentance precedes a blessed life.
5) Those who dismiss Christ sport the colors of the opposing camp.
6) God says Jesus is the Christ; but the fool's head shakes from side to side.
7) Fools prefer choices; but for the righteous, one God is enough.
8) The simple reject the simple way, but the wise aren't seduced by many choices.
9) Faith unlocks heaven's door; but doubt bolts it shut.
10) The Messiah came from God; where are you coming from?

11) Get in step with Christ if you want to walk with God.

12) I give you a riddle to ponder, a puzzle to be solved: Do fools reject the Righteous One of God because they are fools, or are they fools because they reject the Righteous one?

13) Do believers accept Jesus as the Christ because they are believers, or are they believers because they accept Jesus as the Son of God?

14) Fools who fight the cause of Christ invite calamity upon themselves.

15) A good relationship with God's children demands a personal relationship with God's Son.

16) A relationship with God is fellowship with the Son, and fellowship with the Son is a timeless life of God's love.

Dear Lord, Forgive me when I accept you mentally, emotionally, and spiritually, while denying you with my actions. Amen.

CHAPTER 18

A LIFE OF PROMISE

> See that what you have heard from the beginning remains in you. If it does, you also will remain in the Son and in the Father. And this is what he promised us—even eternal life. **1 John 2:24–25 NIV**

1) Loving grace and a forgiving spirit are trademarks of our loving God.
2) False teachings choke the truth like weeds crowding out grass.
3) Let God's love be a welcomed guest in your home.
4) Doubters share their pit of despair, but the righteous share salvation's Son.
5) Sit with God in the morning and learn from Him all day long.
6) Jesus built a wall that separates us from sin, but fools climb the wall in a quest for fun.
7) The philosophy of men is but a bar of soap that washes the skin but not the soul.
8) Sin can put an end to us, but Christ can put an end to sin.
9) Listen to the right gospel to become the right person.

10) Having become the right person, the right life should now be lived.

11) As a vise grips steel, the redeemed cling to truth.

12) To reject part of Christ is to reject all of God.

13) Seekers pass the well of life in their search for truth.

14) Those who don't dilute the Words of Christ are themselves not easily deluded.

15) Neither lock the windows of your mind open, nor bolt the doors of your heart shut.

16) Beware of lessons for losing; they are of the adversary's choosing.

17) Let Him who dwelt among us live within us.

18) Don't let hell's heat melt your Christian convictions.

19) By no means can we be a means of mercy for our own sin.

20) The promises of Christ are co-signed by God.

21) Jesus paved the road to heaven; then He paid our toll.

22) The truth about Jesus is God's truth.

23) Sin is not a good thing, even when it is a fun thing.

Dear Lord, I have heard the truth. Bolster my faith, strength and commitment so that I remain true to it. Amen.

CHAPTER 19
SEDUCERS

> I am writing these things to you about those who are trying to lead you astray. As for you, the anointing you received from Him remains in you, and you do not need anyone to teach you. But as His anointing teaches you about all things and as that anointing is real, not counterfeit— just as it has taught you, remain in Him. **1 John 2:26–27 NIV**

1) Blend many religions and brew a poisonous tea.
2) Misdirection and sleight of tongue are tricks of the deceiver's trade.
3) Beware of confidence men who lure with lies and numb the mind with ritual and comfort.
4) Enticing teachings awaken our dreams and tease us away from the safety of His truth.
5) Enjoy make-believe; employ true belief; and hold fast to your faith.
6) A drop of poison pollutes a pond; and a twist of words contaminates truth.
7) Gossip is juicier than a ripe apple, and provocative ideas can be more exciting than truth.
8) Religious seducers smirk in the dark.

9) Faith gives birth to faith, but fake doctrine buries believers alive.

10) God anoints, man appoints, but fools pour oil upon their own head.

11) The open-minded are easily seduced, but the true believer is rarely deceived.

12) The righteous are anointed with God's truth, but the self-righteous appoint themselves as gods.

13) An all-pleasant god is best suited to hang from a mirror; but an all-present God is to be revered above all.

14) Situational and relevant values float softly onto our minds, but God's commandments fall hard on soft teachings.

15) Stories from the imagination pretend and fantasize; but the story of the cross never double-crosses the truth.

16) A closed Bible cannot speak; a silent preacher cannot be heard; but those who know His word sing songs of hope to a world in despair.

17) As sugar rots a tooth, lies will decay the heart.

18) Candy from strangers spoils an appetite for truth.

19) Soft-selling hard truth produces shallow faith.

20) Absolute truth is sometimes harder to swallow than sugar-coated lies.

21) Those who seek God's anointing are rarely disappointed.

22) Lies left parked in truth's garage soon receive a permanent pass.

23) False seeds are planted in God's garden when we deceive our children with make-believe.

24) Like sharp and pointed toys, perverted teachings threaten God's children.

25) Like metal to a magnet, the unwary are drawn to easy answers.

26) Before plain truth races against exciting ideas, be sure you're playing on a level field.

27) Beware of those who dilute the truth, pollute with words, and seduce with false promises.

28) God's anointing may cause friction while separating fact from fiction.

29) When good ideas argue with scripture, bad ideas are born.

30) Those who pervert scripture stab a knife into God's heart.

31) Unswerving feet rest upon God's Word.

32) The anointed are God's appointed.

33) They who search His Word for truth know He's true to His Word.

Dear Lord, sharpen my awareness against false teachings so that I immediately recognize them for what they are. Amen.

CHAPTER 20

NOW AND THEN

> And now, dear children, continue in Him, so that when He appears we may be confident and unashamed before Him at His coming. If you know that He is righteous, you know that everyone who does what is right has been born of Him. **1 John 2:28–29 NIV**

1) An uncommitted artist draws scorn.
2) Those who are proud of their humility have nothing to brag about.
3) Spontaneous righteousness points to God.
4) A straddled fence blocks conviction.
5) A vacillating faith is afraid of the dark.
6) Shame comes to those who boast.
7) Our roller coaster faith is nauseating to God.
8) The righteous survive, skeptics dive, and scoffers see no higher than their feet.
9) God turns runts into giants.
10) Survive and stay alive through Christ.
11) True piety doesn't recognize its own righteousness.
12) Stand tall, don't fall; be firm, don't squirm; pray more, be more.

13) Like the maple leaf in autumn, the self-righteous can be beautiful before they fall.

14) Continued acts of righteousness are the children of obedience.

15) Those ashamed of their faith have little faith to be ashamed of.

16) We can only stand with Him then by standing for Him now.

17) Dirty feet and inflated egos both soil what they touch.

18) Pompous pride camouflages a puny faith.

19) Do unto Jesus what you would have Him do unto you.

20) Make random goodness your regular habit.

21) Let acts of righteousness be synonymous with your name.

22) Blessed are those who have a working faith; their faith is the work of God.

Dear Lord, I have a low confidence level because my righteousness is low. I will lean on your righteousness and place my confidence in you. Amen.

CHAPTER 21

NEITHER HIM NOR US

> How great is the love the Father has lavished on us, that we should be called children of God! And that is what we are! The reason the world does not know us is that it did not know Him. **1 John 3:1 NIV**

1) Learn the secret of love from Jesus.
2) Loving us is God's choice; but loving Him is ours.
3) Jesus is our frame of reference for the Father's love; and the picture within the frame is painted with a forgiving hand.
4) How quickly our love flips from sunshine to shun-mine; but God's love always hums the same tune.
5) God's love is foreign to the world, but the world's love is foreign to few.
6) Fools refuse to meet God, but the righteous know the beat of His heart.
7) Like bees to nectar, the wounded are drawn to God's healing love.
8) God adopts the humble, but the proud remain orphans all their days.
9) Few believers act like children of God, but many act like children.

10) Many will proclaim our devilish ways, but a family resemblance to Christ is viewed through squinted eyes.

11) Many are those who attack God's love when they should be attracted to it.

12) Our need for love is as boundless as our Father's love for us.

13) It is better to experience the love of God than to understand it.

14) Intellectuals must understand God's love before they accept it; but the wise accept it before attempting to understand it.

15) Like wisps of smoke is a mother's affection compared to the love God has for us.

16) God doesn't love us because He needs us; He loves us because He wants to.

17) The entire world is desperate for a love that God isn't obligated to give.

18) People of the world should meet the God of heaven and earth.

19) God's unconditional love reaches out to draw us in.

20) By the time parents understand parenthood, their children are grown.

21) Folks often appreciate childhood more than they appreciated being children.

22) It is better to be born-again late in life than to be late being born again.

23) God's children love their siblings.

Dear Lord, increase my awareness of your love, so that my love will be more obvious to others. Amen.

CHAPTER 22

CHILDREN, GROW UP

> Dear friends, now we are children of God, and what we will be has not yet been made known. But we know that when He appears, we shall be like Him, for we shall see Him as He is. Everyone who has this hope in Him purifies himself, just as He is pure. **1 John 3:2–3 NIV**

1) As a reflection reverses the truth, our minds revise the facts.
2) Hope without Christ is like fire without heat.
3) A life committed to Christ is a life laced with hope.
4) Maturity walks heaven's streets.
5) God's children should grow up.
6) Jesus gives hope, and hope follows behind our Lord.
7) Complete trust in God leaves no room to trust another.
8) We haven't met tomorrow; but we spent today with Christ; and yesterday's memories are warmed by His love.
9) Today we don't know what our whole life with God will be like, but we should know what today with Christ was like.

10) The wise draw inspiration from heaven's well, but the short-sighted soon drain their own cistern dry.

11) Righteousness is born in the heart and nurtured in the mind.

12) Like the flight of a sparrow, our purity rises and falls.

13) Sometimes children's destiny can only be apparent to their parent.

14) What we'll be like in heaven is but a guess while we're still here.

15) It is better to be small with a tall faith than to be tall with a small faith.

16) Everyone who ignores Christ hops through life on one foot.

17) Peace prevails when heaven's hope warms our heart.

18) Hope in Christ is a purifying hope, and a purifying hope nudges us closer to Him.

Dear Lord, make me more aware that my hope and trust is in you. Amen.

CHAPTER 23

SIN NO MORE

> Everyone who sins breaks the law; in fact, sin is lawlessness. But you know that he appeared so that he might take away our sins. And in him is no sin. No one who lives in him keeps on sinning. No one who continues to sin has either seen him or known him. **1 John 3: 4–6 NIV**

1) Sliding back into sin is a downhill trip, but climbing out is an uplifting experience.
2) The fool believes that outward change is the first step to a righteous life.
3) Sin is life without God, and life without Christ gives a clear view of hell.
4) The forgiven dump their sin onto loving hands; and the victorious stay clean by the grace of God.
5) Those who live outside of God's law wrestle demons in their sleep.
6) Christians don't deliberately slip and fall, but they slip just the same.
7) Jesus is sin-free, but we only imagine we are.
8) Because all sin, few believe that life can be different.
9) The forgiven aren't immune to new sin, but Christ can arrest the sinning nature.

10) All who ascend to the mountain with the Lord will descend to the valley with a new name.

11) It is better to live the life of a frog than to continue to drown in unbelief.

12) Why stand outside looking in, when you could be inside with a Savior who looks out for you.

13) Faith lasts as long as a hummingbird's song for those who adjust their convictions to fit the situation.

14) Does anyone desire to become a house of God? Then live inside of the love of Christ.

15) Who can walk with the divine? Who will be invited to enter His presence? Confessing mouths, believing hearts, and unworthy souls who depend upon Him.

16) It is better to ride in the saddle with Jesus than to enter life's rodeo alone.

17) Houses built inside God's garden are surrounded with a glorious view.

18) The lawlessness of sin isn't the work of a flawless Christ.

19) The gutter has no lasting grip on those who hold His hand.

20) Unpraying lips don't ride above a believing heart.

21) Step inside of God's will with a believer's foot.

22) We are a lawless people in need of a divine lawyer.

23) To stroll with Jesus one must walk away from sin.

24) Change with Christ by being changed by Christ.

25) God's way becomes our way when our way gives way to His.

26) Though you run from sin, sin still lurks in the dark.

Dear Lord, I pray that I will keep depending upon you instead of myself. Remind me that this is what I really want and need. Amen.

CHAPTER 24

God's Seeds Yield Good Fruit

> Dear children, do not let anyone lead you astray. He who does what is right is righteous, just as He is righteous. He who does what is sinful is of the devil, because the devil has been sinning from the beginning. The reason the Son of God appeared was to destroy the devil's work. No one who is born of God will continue to sin, because God's seed remains in him; he cannot go on sinning, because he has been born of God. **1 John 3:7–9 NIV**

1) Fruit drops from its own branch.
2) God's empowerment grows one trust at a time.
3) Only the confused would refuse adoption into God's family.
4) The Holy Spirit of God locks no one in darkness.
5) Juice can't spill from the glass it's not in.
6) The insecure follow the "thought du jour," and the noncommitted are never secure.
7) Ducks don't grow hair, and the devil can't wear God's clothes.
8) When the deceived enter a fiery path, they are soon overcome by smoke.
9) Milk spoils only once; but people aren't milk.

10) A child follows the role model it's given; but an adult follows the one it chooses.

11) An evening walk in sin; a morning jog from God.

12) Sin and Christ don't ride the same train; but they desire to train the same people.

13) Neither the sinning nor the dying want to be alone.

14) Though the born-again sin anew; forgiveness is their most cherished gift.

15) Sin's red-lit door still holds allure for the forgiven who've forgotten His name.

16) Doctored doctrines and deceived deceivers create betrayed believers.

17) Twice born is heaven; once born is hell.

18) All God's adopted haven't adapted to being royalty.

19) Spiritual schizophrenics occupy both bar and pew.

20) New wine won't taste like old grape juice.

21) The leader of defeat is the king of lies; and the liar king cons even the wise.

Dear Lord, You alone are righteous. I pray that I always remember this reality, knowing that I need Your help day by day and hour by hour. Amen

CHAPTER 25

NO LIES

> This is how we know who the children of God are and who the children of the devil are: Anyone who does not do what is right is not a child of God; neither is anyone who does not love his brother. **1 John 3:10 NIV**

1) God's love flows in His children's veins.
2) All the roses in the garden won't change a skunk's scent.
3) The olive grove accepts no plow, and the barren ground needs no harvest.
4) Ravens don't fly with cardinals, and their song is never as sweet.
5) A weevil loves cotton and a liar loves to weave; but the righteous don't destroy their own home.
6) A wolf's teeth were not made for grass.
7) God's children love the dawn; but the devil's kids love the night.
8) The righteous love easily, but the self-righteous love to judge.
9) A loving church spreads its love, but a dying church loves itself.

10) Greedy weeds love the farmer when he fertilizes the field, but they hate the hands that clear the way for crops to grow.

11) The righteous love to pray, but the contentious love to argue.

12) Though the devil's kind denies their dad, the resemblance increases day by day.

13) Dissention is a boiling pot too close to the baby's bed.

14) The difference between the good and the just is the God they serve.

15) It's easier to cuddle an angry dog than to live with a faultfinder.

16) Of what use is righteousness to those who loathe its fruits? Of what gain is good when God has left the room?

17) Like hot soup on a cold day is the loving fellowship of Christian friends.

18) While the rich despise taxes, the poor rejoice in sharing bread.

19) Though weeds grow among the crops, they provide nothing for the harvest.

20) It is better to fight with a tiger than to pretend to be a child of God.

21) Like rust on a pipe is a sister who refuses love.

22) Like elephants among cattle, God's children are easily seen.

23) Evil is the devil's child, and the devil has many children.

24) As a fire destroys both animal and tree, evil devours both sinner and saint.

25) When the best of the worst resembles the best of the best, the wise pray for discernment.

26) The farmer who sows hate is soon entangled by the vindictive briars he plants.

27) Rotten meat won't make good stew.

28) Stony fields grow skinny flocks.

29) Closet Christians with glass doors soon become transparent.

30) A healthy church is a healing church.

31) An angry bull scatters the herd.

32) An unloving sister remains an only child.

Dear Lord, I pray that I will always be proud to be your child. Amen.

CHAPTER 26
HATE

> This is the message you heard from the beginning: We should love one another. Do not be like Cain, who belonged to the evil one and murdered his brother. And why did he murder him? Because his own actions were evil and his brother's were righteous. Do not be surprised, my brothers, if the world hates you. **1 John 3:11–13 NIV**

1) Live love and give love, and you will be loved.
2) Hate opens the door to evil, and evil quickly scoots in.
3) The loved live to love, but the hated hate to live.
4) Live to love and love to live, but hate to hate without loving to hate.
5) The wise don't give in to hate, but fools don't give in to love.
6) Righteousness is admired, but seldom respected; and goodness is respected from afar.
7) The seeds of Cain may sleep in our hearts, but without nurture their crops soon fail.
8) Bad news makes headlines, but good news is page nine.
9) The hate that separated Cain from his brother easily separates us from ours.

10) As a broken string shatters the violin's harmony, quarrelling tongues shred the church's unity.

11) As Abel's goodness was despised by his brother, righteousness draws the unbeliever's scorn.

12) Like acid in water, hate pollutes a sea of love.

13) It is better to be inspired by the righteous than to be admired by the earth's underbelly.

14) He who goes spoiling for a fight spoils the air he breathes.

15) Righteousness reveals the emptiness of selfish goodness.

16) Hate is a handle on evil's door.

17) Inspiration from the righteousness of others leads to an inspiring life.

18) Follow Christ, not Cain.

19) The light of righteousness illuminates evil.

20) Like a jealous brother, the world belittles the Christian.

21) "Always" and "Almost" play together well, until "Adversity" joins the fun.

22) Peas in a pod are too close to fight.

23) Beware of Cain; he kills and disables the Able he is unable to outdo.

24) Don't raise cane; Cain razed Able.

Dear Lord, I know that ill feelings toward my brothers and sisters in Christ separate me from You as well as them. Alert me when I harbor feelings that damage our relationship. Amen.

CHAPTER 27

WE KNOW

> We know that we have passed from death to life, because we love our brothers. Anyone who does not love remains in death. Anyone who hates his brother is a murderer, and you know that no murderer has eternal life in him. This is how we know what love is: Jesus Christ laid down his life for us. And we ought to lay down our lives for our brothers. **1 John 3:14–16 NIV**

1) Hate eats our hearts, but love feeds our soul.
2) Hate's fingers and the mortician's hands make death's handshake firm.
3) Love gives life, and a loving life gives joy.
4) Like a hawk floating in the sky; dissention searches for emissaries.
5) Hatred hates love.
6) God's love is a tough love, but ours is paper easily torn.
7) Hatred murders, but love resurrects.
8) Christ's love reaches deep and spreads far.
9) Like a worm eating an apple, hate devours from the inside out.
10) It is easier for a butterfly to reenter its cocoon than it is for bitterness to sweeten one's faith.

11) It is easier to love many than to forgive one.

12) God's love knows neither boundaries nor barriers.

13) When the hated dies, the hater grins.

14) Like a bombing jet sowing destruction, hate is ready to rejoice in its kills.

15) Love in our hearts brings love into our home.

16) Hard feelings come from a hardened heart.

17) Love minus forgiveness flies a false flag.

18) Hate is the father of hurt.

19) Without love, we're leaves on a tree, waiting to fall.

20) Abundant life is a loving gift from a loving God.

21) Love grounded in feeling is a fleeting love, but love running to God is well grounded.

22) Hate does not express Christ's love any more than God's love expresses devilish hate.

23) Christ shares no room with hatred; and hatred shares nothing.

Dear Lord, I don't want to be a murderer in my heart. Deliver me from hate. Amen.

CHAPTER 28

PASSION AND COMPASSION

> If anyone has material possessions and sees his brother in need but has no pity on him, how can the love of God be in him? Dear children, let us not love with words or tongue but with actions and in truth. **1 John 3:17–18 NIV**

1) God's love isn't cheap; it is free.
2) God's work demands overtime.
3) Talking tongues tell tall tales; but holy hands hurry to help.
4) Give and it will be given to you; take and it will be taken from you.
5) Love with deeds, indeed; do right with might; be good for God; and do your due.
6) Store love and compassion with priceless possessions; and then live with the door open.
7) To give is to live; to merely try is to die.
8) God is the author of life, but few credit Him for His work.
9) Harmonize lazy hands with a believing heart.
10) It is better to sift God's love through uncertain fingers than to live in fear of being thought a fool.
11) Put love in your wallet, and then set it free.

12) These three work together as one: Pity leads, compassion follows, and action gives them life.

13) Righteousness weeps at the world's hurts and then sets eager hands to do what its heart feels.

14) Express holy passion with godly compassion.

15) My child, if you wish to better your world, this you must do: Do all you can do and go until you can go no further; then step beyond your ambition into God's world.

16) Do more than teach. Reach.

17) Do more than talk. Walk.

18) Do more than sing. Bring.

19) Do more than read. Lead.

20) Do more than stay. Pray.

21) Do more than no. Know.

22) Do more than live. Give.

23) Do more than yelp. Help.

24) Do more than cry. Buy.

25) Do more than die. Try.

26) Do more than lose. Choose.

27) Do more than sleep. Weep.

28) Do more than rest. Bless.

29) Do more than raze. Praise.

30) Do more than observe. Preserve.

31) Do more than object. Protect.

32) Do more than study. Buddy.

33) Do more than remonstrate. Demonstrate.

Dear Lord, open my heart and my hands. Direct my mind and my manners. Open my passion and my compassion. Direct my will and my way. Amen.

CHAPTER 29

HISTORY OR HIS STORY?

> Dear children, let us not love with words or tongue but with actions and in truth. This then is how we know that we belong to the truth, and how we set our hearts at rest in His presence whenever our hearts condemn us. For God is greater than our hearts, and He knows everything. **1 John 3:18–20 NIV**

1) Fire the agent who specializes in guilt trips.
2) Poison oozes from lying lips.
3) Confidence comes when belief and actions swing from the same trapeze.
4) Beware if you start to like the noise when your heart and convictions sing out of tune.
5) Write your songs in notes of conviction, and sing them loudly by living the words.
6) Make both history and convictions one long chapter in your life's story.
7) Words may begin the task, but conviction brings completion.
8) What we say eschews our values, but what we do displays our ways.
9) Words may wind the key and cheers may tease us into action, but commitment powers the train.

10) Actions may speak louder than feelings; but feelings howl throughout the night.

11) Shadows of history correct the course, but words from peers condemn their own.

12) Many critical spirits wear a cross.

13) Talking to God without following your faith is talking trash to God.

14) Make your hands back up your words.

15) Live love and love to live; give love and love to give.

16) All who stand in His shadow rest in His presence.

17) It is better to pray quietly with your actions than to lead congregations with flowery prayers.

18) Those who speak loving words from an empty heart sow disappointment in a field of dreams.

19) Live love, give love, and be loved; feel the warmth of God's smile.

20) An unloving person turns beautiful words into trash-mail.

21) The fool listens to a heart that argues with God.

22) A lying tongue betrays a cold heart.

23) Loving tongues don't make promises the hands can't keep.

24) Lazy hands with loving mouths bring disgrace upon their house.

Dear Lord, I pray that I will be more in your eyes than in mine. Amen.

CHAPTER 30

CONFIDENT PRAYERS

> Dear friends, if our hearts do not condemn us, we have confidence before God and receive from Him anything we ask, because we obey His commands and do what pleases Him. **1 John 3:21–22 NIV**

1) A hardened heart seeks proof, not pleas.
2) Self-condemnation mires holy feet in mud.
3) Love is blind, faith needs no eyes, and prayer sees eternal hope.
4) Doubters dwell on their past mistakes and failures, but believers remember God's faithfulness to their obedience.
5) Prayer shapes the future and the past fuels the present; but the truth builds people of God.
6) Forgotten acts of goodness invite termites into a house of prayer.
7) The merciless laugh as the fishermen fight the ocean's vicious waves, but the compassionate help bail their battered boats and pull their tattered nets.
8) A condemning heart demands death, but a forgiving God grants full pardon.
9) Crying over spilt guilt deepens its grip, but giving it to God releases its grasp.

10) The faithful pray to a faithful God; but when the faithless fall, who is there to lift them up?

11) What God forgives He remembers no more, but the human memory is never so kind.

12) Prayer warriors live to do God's will, but spectators only pray in the presence of pain.

13) The strong count their losses before they begin and remember their wins after the war.

14) Forgiveness holds no hostages with guns of guilt, but a condemning heart refuses to let us go.

15) It is easier to sunbathe in a bed of ants than to live with a condemning spouse.

16) Three things I know: These four have I seen: Laziness creates beggars; dishonesty spawns liars; selfish prayers soon turn to wishes; and Godly obedience turns dwarfs into giants.

17) One word from God heals a thousand hurts.

18) It is better to swim in a pond of faithfulness than to be buried in a grave of gold.

19) Three things God loves; even four does He cherish: A clear conscience, an active hand, a strong faith, and a desire to be like Jesus.

20) When right seems wrong, we turn bread into stone. When wrong seems right, we eat stones in the night.

21) The righteous walk the dusty roads with Jesus.

22) A condemning heart quickly turns into a hanging judge.

23) Prayers clear the ceiling of those with a clear conscience toward God.

24) As we avoid what God forbids, our prayers gain confidence.

25) The power of forgiven guilt fades as memory gives it life.

26) Bold prayers come from forgiving hearts.

27) Happy are those who go to God for a cleansing shower.

28) To stand before God, one must kneel in prayer.

29) To walk with Jesus, one must sit at His feet.

30) To run with angels, one must step with forgiveness.

31) When the faithful pray, their prayers are faithfully answered.

32) Self-loathing prevents self-loving, and self-loving evicts a condemning heart.

33) I have no trouble remembering my mistakes, but I tend to forget that I have done some things right.

Dear Lord, please bring to mind those things I have been doing right, and those actions I should continue to do and improve upon. Amen.

CHAPTER 31
MUTUAL TENANTS

> And this is His command: to believe in the name of His Son, Jesus Christ, and to love one another as He commanded us. Those who obey His commands live in Him, and He in them. And this is how we know that He lives in us: We know it by the Spirit He gave us. **1 John 3:23–24 NIV**

1) Let God in on your identity crisis.
2) God comes to us by invitation, and He stays because we accept His terms.
3) Our bodies need nourishment, our souls need Christ; and our spirit needs them both.
4) I offered God a one-way ticket to my thrown-away life, and He welcomed me back from the dead.
5) God maintains His presence within the obedient.
6) Christ is not a secret to be kept.
7) Love and obedience are paternal twins.
8) A demanding love is driven by need; but unconditional love is empowered by God.
9) Godly love is freely given; additional requirements alter love's name.
10) True believers love without bias, but pseudo-saints select without shame.

11) The wise have Christ in their home from the days of their youth, but fools don't speak His Holy name until their house is falling down.

12) The Lord God may oft be silent, but still He makes His presence known.

13) God speaks, but few are tuned to the right frequency.

14) Without air we have no life; without God we have no air.

15) It is easier for a trout to swim to the stars than for God to remain in the heart of a bigot.

16) Believers hear God speak and crawl inside His Word to rest.

17) The day a daisy is a radio host is the day our hearts will need no love.

18) Why does God's Spirit make Himself known? Because He wants us to know He is near.

19) Three things God abhors, even four does He despise: Hearts that hate, lips that lie, hands that hit, and spirits that set themselves against Christ.

20) As a preacher shuns gossip, the haughty avoid God's Word.

21) Believers who live out their beliefs are living in God's Spirit.

22) Fools who set their Bibles on fire set their soul aflame.

23) Like Father, like Son. Love Father, Love Son.

24) Contingency clauses don't belong in a "love contract."

25) Live in Him the way air flows in you.

26) A self-righteous foot will trample on God's toes.

27) Air not breathed through prayer soon goes stale.

28) Believe and love, and love to believe.

29) Love the God you believe in, and believe in the God you love.

30) Experience God to the fullest by being fully His.

31) Love the Father; love the Son. Trust the Son; trust the Father.

32) Disobedient feet run from God.

Dear Lord, reveal yourself by your spirit, and may my Christianity be revealed by my actions. Amen.

CHAPTER 32

FALSE PROPHETS

> Dear friends, do not believe every spirit, but test the spirits to see whether they are from God, because many false prophets have gone out into the world. **1 John 4:1 NIV**

1) Good credentials are not always a guarantee of quality.
2) Let the true testimony of Jesus be the test for all teachings.
3) Truth and God's Word proceed from the Master's mouth.
4) Teachings that dump the humanity of Jesus are at home in a dump.
5) The spirit of tolerance for all religions is intolerable to God.
6) Teaching about God and being godly are as alike as clouds and wind.
7) Truth builds its foundation on God's Son and builds its proof in Mary's Son.
8) A closing of the Bible, a glance away from the Lord, and a soul is lost in the fog.
9) Obedient believers refuse notions that dilute their faith.
10) The faithful rise from their slumber to kneel in prayer, but the lazy continue to snore.

11) The confused seek God who is out there somewhere, but the wise place their trust in the Christ who came here.

12) God is spirit, but no other spirits are God.

13) Religions and philosophies dance to many tunes, but Jesus played only one.

14) False messages give false answers to the question of who Jesus was.

15) It is better to gain limited knowledge than to have an abundance of possibilities and a scarcity of solutions.

16) Not all spiritual teachings were born in Bethlehem, laid in a manger, and nailed to a cross.

17) Some fools keep the windows of their mind forever jammed open, while others are sure to lock theirs shut.

18) Lilies radiate their beauty in the light of the sun; gold proclaims its value to all who listen; but the wisdom of the world bears its ugliness in light of the truth.

19) The man who walked on water also walked on land; and the man who fed the five thousand also ate. The man who walked the earth left His footprints; and the man who fed the thousands still feeds the millions.

20) If a spirit of truth refutes the truth about Christ; then the truth is that that spirit is not the spirit of God.

21) Pseudo-intellectuals respect His teachings while rejecting His teacher; and the deluded world proclaims the ignorant to be experts in their field.

22) False messages and rhetorical proofs are spoofs that deny the truth of who Jesus was.

Dear Lord, help me inventory my beliefs and discard those not powered by your Spirit. Amen.

CHAPTER 33

WHO IS THE ANTICHRIST?

> But every spirit that does not acknowledge Jesus is not from God. This is the spirit of the antichrist, which you have heard is coming and even now is already in the world. **1 John 4:3 NIV**

1) The antichrists may outwardly display respect for the Jesus they inwardly reject.
2) Ignoring the one we love is a step in the direction of rejection.
3) A half-truth is a Christless truth.
4) A good message without Jesus is a bad message.
5) Steer clear of being nearly here.
6) God gave Jesus a round-trip ticket.
7) Reject Christ and blaze a trail for the antichrist.
8) Straddle the fence and become an antichrist by default.
9) Discard the Son's ID card, and throw away Jesus.
10) Fools get on the wrong team by making the wrong choice; and skeptics are on the wrong side by making no choice.

11) Good messages and God-messages often wear the same clothes.

12) Those not for Christ are against Christ, and those standing for nothing will not be standing in the end.

13) Those against Christ and those without an opinion are skin on the same bones.

14) Choose the Cross-road; put purpose in your life.

15) Jesus is from God; many deny it. But tell the fools their horoscope, and stupidly, they buy it.

16) The antichrists proclaim god by many names, but God claims these proclaimers by none.

17) Beware of seekers who acknowledge the goodness of Jesus but not the God-ness of Jesus.

18) Antichrist tailors dress Jesus in many suits with matching religious ties.

19) False teachers may appear pro-Christ, but only preach half of Him.

20) The spirit of the deceiver is against what it should be for.

21) She who worships a Godless Christ sports a triangle that is round.

22) A Christless gospel is a crisis gospel.

23) It is best to remain unborn than to refuse to be born again.

24) Jesus is our Godsend, because God sent us Jesus.

25) The Holy One became our neighbor in order to become our champion.

26) Beware of those that proclaim Jesus to be one prophet among many.

27) If you are led to believe that Jesus is not from God, then who is leading you?

28) Beware of shallow thinkers who are deep expounders.

29) Many who claim to be driven away from God are their own chauffeur.

Dear Lord, I pray that I will always accept the total You. Amen.

CHAPTER 34

WHO HEARS YOU?

> They are from the world and therefore speak from the viewpoint of the world, and the world listens to them. We are from God, and whoever knows God listens to us; but whoever is not from God does not listen to us. This is how we recognize the Spirit of truth and the spirit of falsehood. **1 John 4:5–6 NIV**

1) Twisted truth nudges the naive from their faith.
2) The antichrist dresses in chameleon clothes.
3) They remain godless who reject His Word.
4) Beware of the smart without a heart.
5) Dusty Bibles remain silent.
6) Evade the confusion sown by fault-finding farmers.
7) Skeptical souls search for faith in an empty maze of darkness.
8) Don't force God into your box of beliefs.
9) God listens when we talk, but we talk when we should listen.
10) Chocolate melts, wood burns, and an adverse spirit destroy the soul.

11) The spirit of God and the spirit of Christ neither argue nor enter into dispute.

12) Lift His amazing grace to your parched lips, and quench the amazing thirst of your dry soul.

13) Christ's followers cherish God's Word, but His Word means nothing to those with hardened hearts.

14) God without Christ is like a body without a heart.

15) Those of God, listen to God.

16) Christ's words are meaningful for those to whom Christ is meaningful.

17) Jesus then; Jesus now.

18) They who don't understand Jesus won't understand His followers.

19) Walk not in the ways of an agnostic, nor have tea with a hungry bear.

20) What Jesus called truth, the pious called lies.

21) As the caterpillar weaves its cocoon, the master liar envelops the mind.

22) Like the hunter in a tree, satan centers his crosshairs on his prey.

23) As a child shrieks at a clown, the cynic howls at the minister's words.

24) The logician postulates, the magician levitates, and the world reasons away the truth.

25) Read God's good news before reading the bad news in the morning.

Dear Lord, keep me spiritually alert so that I will not follow the antichrist while thinking I am following you. Amen.

CHAPTER 35

LOVE

> Dear friends, let us love one another, for love comes from God. Everyone who loves has been born of God and knows God. Whoever does not love does not know God, because God is love. **1 John 4:7–8 NIV**

1) God's love never cheats.
2) A non-loving person has never shaken hands with Jesus.
3) A compassionate love is a passionate love.
4) A forgiving love has already been given.
5) God's love has an iron grip.
6) God's love defies definition.
7) An empty purse sells the kind of love that money can buy.
8) Love comes from God and must be returned.
9) Mankind's love seeks to be fair but doesn't know how.
10) God is love, but love is not God.
11) The way to a fool's heart is through passion; but the way to God's heart is through compassion.
12) God sees though our manipulative plans and plots, but God's love sees us through.

13) God's love doesn't help us to escape sorrow, but it gets us through it.

14) The belligerent bully demands to be loved, but has no love to give.

15) Unforgiving people readily accept a forgiveness they can never give.

16) God's love sees us through, even though He sees through us.

17) Those who love the Lord but reject fellow believers are really the object of their own love.

18) When you enter into God's house, bring a bundle of love for each one there.

19) God's people reach out to all as if their hands were His hands.

20) As the rain falls on the just and the unjust, God's love descends softly upon our shoulders, massaging our battered souls with fragrant oils and soothing grace.

21) To know God without knowing love is as easy as swimming naked without getting wet.

22) An all-giving love can only be given by God.

23) Love from on high is beyond marvelous, so how can we understand it?

24) To sing in God's choir, one must sing songs of love.

25) We hasten to our loving God in fear of the dark void of the devil's den.

26) Without Your love, O God, we are but bags of flesh filled with foul breath.

27) A recipe for a changed life: In a cold heart, combine God's unlimited compassion, a generous amount of heavenly hope, and a bottomless bowl of His amazing grace laced with eternal forgiveness, and God's love will make it warm.

28) Down in the valley all will be well as long as all is well; but when the floods come, all will look unto the hills.

29) The self-righteous use their passion as a con.

30) When God starts the process of our being born again, abortion is never an option.

31) God's love reaches farther than anyone has ever gone, except one.

32) Counterfeit love bickers and quarrels for the joy of a struggle, and wannabe love goes begging for a fight.

33) God's love is neither a pushover nor to be walked over. His love is sometimes meek, but never weak.

34) When love's cup is overflowing with bickering and quarreling, the cup has no room for love.

35) More than a good thing, love is a God-thing.

36) Those who don't know God, don't know enough.

Dear Lord, teach me how to love without manipulation, and how to be compassionate without being gullible. Teach me to love while being firm, and to be meek while being strong. Amen.

CHAPTER 36

AT-ONE-NESS

> This is how God showed His love among us: He sent his one and only Son into the world that we might live through Him. This is love: not that we loved God, but that He loved us and sent His Son as an atoning sacrifice for our sins. **1 John 4:9–10 NIV**

1) God's light shines through Jesus' hands and feet.
2) Life without God is a living death.
3) The map to heaven has but one road.
4) The uniqueness of Jesus is more than the lessons He taught.
5) Jesus gives us "at-one-ment" with God.
6) Ornate sacks filled with air give no nourishment; and love songs alone starve a hungry heart.
7) Our love for God proves nothing; but His love for us proves everything.
8) The devil counterfeits God's love, and the fake is sometimes discovered too late.
9) Looking for God is not so hard; accepting Christ is not complex; but living for Jesus is not always easy.
10) The merciless say to their unborn child, "You die!" but the merciful tell their child being born, "Now live!"

11) A spirit-filled life is a loving life.
12) Satan is pro-life; his! Jesus is pro-life; ours!
13) When asked to choose between life and death, the selfish ask, "Whose"?
14) When asked to jot what God says write, the forgiven asks, "What?"
15) When asked to begin what God wants done, the selfless asks, "When?"
16) When asked to share His love with others, the godly asks, "Where?"
17) When asked to cry what God wants said, the skeptic asks, "Why?"
18) Inner peace is as long as a butterfly's life for those not at peace with God.
19) Three things amaze me. Even four cause me awe: Hibernating bears in their winter caves, snoozing roses in frozen ground, an eclipsing sun at high noon, and Jesus rising from the Grave.
20) Compared to the resurrection power of Christ, black holes are as but leopard spots on a synthetic rug.
21) Love demonstrated is sometime hated.
22) In search of evidence of a creator, I looked up at the universe. In search of evidence of my need for forgiveness, I looked down at myself. In search of evidence of God's love, I looked back at the cross. In search of evidence of God's grace, I looked ahead to the judgment.

Dear Lord, I sometimes emphasize your teachings so much that I forget what you did. Keep the whole truth ever before me. Amen.

CHAPTER 37

LOVE TO US, IN US, AND FROM US

> Dear friends, since God so loved us, we also ought to love one another. No one has ever seen God; but if we love one another, God lives in us and His love is made complete in us. We know that we live in Him and He in us, because He has given us of His Spirit. **1 John 4:11–13 NIV**

1) Let others catch you loving them, and catch others loving you.
2) Our outside reveals our inside.
3) Be different from the ignorant.
4) God is good, and we are grateful.
5) Nothing is as profound as God's love, and nothing as profane as those who don't care.
6) The self-righteous are seen doing selfish things, but the righteous are convicted of committing love.
7) I searched for God with a telescope, but found God's love in a Christian.
8) Searching for truth takes a lifetime; finding Christ takes but a moment.
9) To remain in God is to remain in love.
10) God may be hard to see, but His love in us shouldn't be.

11) Puppy love strikes, then we outgrow it; God's love strokes, and we grow up.

12) It is better to kiss a poisonous snake than to ignore God's love.

13) When Christ knocks, invite Him in; but don't close the blinds to hide your guest.

14) Luscious leaves, nesting birds, and happy squirrels are signs of a healthy tree.

15) Three questions I ask, even four test my wits: Is it better to be like the water that quenches thirst, or the well that provides it? Is it better to be like the harvest that feeds for a season, or the land that hosts many crops? Is it better to be like the seed that grows into a tree, or the tree that produces many seeds? Is it better to be like the pony so loved by a child, or the child who so loves the pony?

16) More questions tiptoe though my mind; there are puzzles that pick my brain: Is an empty well still a well, or is it just a hole? Is unplanted ground still a farm, or just barren land? Is a dead tree still a tree, or just dry wood? Is a dormant believer still a Christian, or just a mouth that knows the words?

17) Giving salvation your name isn't the same as giving your home address.

Dear Lord, make me aware of the needs within my own worship group before I charge off in quest of ways to serve you. Amen.

CHAPTER 38

LIVING IN LOVE

> And we have seen and testify that the Father has sent his Son to be the Savior of the world. If anyone acknowledges that Jesus is the Son of God, God lives in him and he in God. And so we know and rely on the love God has for us. God is love. Whoever lives in love lives in God, and God in him. **1 John 4:14–16 NIV**

1) Jesus rescues M.I.As.
2) Christ was given a nasty assignment: Us.
3) God's affection cures the infection of sin.
4) Jesus: God's emissary, and our sanctuary.
5) The fool believes today and forgets tomorrow, but God's children remember Him all their days.
6) Like the dogwood that blooms in spring is my love for Jesus; but like the flower budding all seasons is His love for me.
7) The fool follows fun; but the forgiven follow faith.
8) Believers come in; but doubters stay out.
9) Nailing Jesus on a cross is our shame; but Jesus leaving the grave is our victory.
10) I pondered life, considered death, and envisioned heaven; then I thought of life again.

11) When faith advances, doubt retreats; but when doubt delivers, faith pays the bill.
12) It is better to place yourself at God's mercy than to rely upon the mercy of your friends.
13) Those who believe that Jesus lived twice can be born twice.
14) Believe in yourself, because He believes in you.
15) Like a cry in the wilderness is the ache of our sin.
16) Jesus reaches out to us like a bloodhound on the trail; but still we try to dodge.
17) To believe in God is to be living in God.
18) Make Jesus visible by being indivisible with Him.
19) God, the law-giver; Jesus, the love-giver.
20) It is better to die once and live twice than to live once and die twice.
21) God's love is ours when our love is His.

O God, I pray that I will never take your love for granted, and that I will never take you for granted. Amen.

CHAPTER 39
WITHOUT FEAR

> Love is made complete among us so that we will have confidence on the day of judgment, because in this world we are like him. There is no fear in love. But perfect love drives out fear, because fear has to do with punishment. The one who fears is not made perfect in love. **1 John 4:17–18 NIV**

1) Perfected love knocks fear on its ear.
2) Let God's gigantic love cast its protecting shadow upon you.
3) God's love doesn't time-share with fear.
4) Fear and fret love to fight, but they never fight to love.
5) Boldness comes from being loved by God and knowing it.
6) Allow God's love to flow through you like water from a spring.
7) God's love can rule where we are, in the same way His love rules where He is.
8) When we stand in God's presence, only His love will keep us from being afraid.
9) Perfect love comes from God, but imperfect love surrounds us.

Dear Lord, grant me the boldness not to worry, and the confidence to love without fear. Amen.

CHAPTER 40

WHERE DOES LOVE COME FROM?

We love because He first loved us. **1 John 4:19 NIV**

1) God loved you before you were you.
2) True love still flows long after it's forgotten.
3) Godless love comes from godless people.
4) Let God's love turn your dry creeks into rising rivers.
5) Live like God loves you.
6) Our love is but a fragrance from His perfect perfume.
7) God's love is not duty-free.
8) Lures with hooks aren't offered with compassion.
9) God's love confounds genius and outstrips imaginations.
10) True love is God-given and compassion driven.
11) Wonder and beauty are the Lord's to give, and love is the bedrock of both.
12) Love from the godless is good, but it is not God's.
13) Much-needed rain gives farmers relief; a newborn child makes a couple proud; and a loving spouse is a gift that keeps on giving.

14) We found Him who wasn't lost; and He found us who were.

15) Love wears gloves when feeding frightened dogs, but it feeds them just the same.

16) God gives love, but we give grief.

17) The wise let go for His love to flow, but stubborn sailors won't release the helm.

18) Become rich; love a bum.

19) His love touches us so that we can touch others.

20) The gift of loving others is our gift from a loving God.

21) Godless love is a like a one-person marriage.

22) It is better to experience one-thousandth of God's love than to know the passion of a thousand lovers.

23) I looked in my wallet for love, and found it empty; I glimpsed into the mind of a scholar, and saw false ideals; I peeped into the soul of a child and found innocence; I searched the heart of God and found a love that would not let me go.

24) I cracked an egg to make a meal; God broke my spirit to make me whole. I raised my self-esteem to have a life. He shattered my pride to make me live. I tasted treachery that made me hate. He touched my heart, and that made me love.

25) As a mother nursing her puppies, God cuddles the faithful.

26) Three things I love; even four make me grin: Budding trees in spring, a full stomach at noon, a baby bearing my name, and a chance to give love away.

27) They who search in vain for love within, leave their Savior out.

28) Love begins in the beginning with God.

29) God's love lasts, but don't be the last to love God.

Dear Lord, love me always, and I pray that I will always love you. Amen.

CHAPTER 41

HATE MAIL TO GOD

> If anyone says, "I love God," yet hates his brother, he is a liar. For anyone who does not love his brother, whom he has seen, cannot love God, whom he has not seen. And he has given us this command: Whoever loves God must also love his brother. **1 John 4:20–21 NIV**

1) The fool speaks in contradictions.
2) God's love doesn't reject.
3) Hate and love can't break bread in peace.
4) Godly love gives birth to brotherly love.
5) Hate's DNA denies holy love as her father.
6) Love yourself through God's eyes.
7) Both Heavenly Father and earthly brother are our next of kin.
8) Love one another the way Christ loves the church, but don't love the church the way you love one another.
9) Love is neither selfish nor brotherless.
10) Those who hate their brother in the Lord hate the Lord in their brother.
11) Love both Father and brother; not one without the other.

12) It is right to love God as your father, because He loves you as His child.

13) As God honors the righteous, the righteous honor others.

14) Does God give wrong answers to those who pray? Does a mother despise her child in times of its need? Should the righteous refuse love to a member of their congregation?

15) My brother was so busy talking to God that he had no time to be my friend.

16) Hate came to dinner in fancy clothes, and love arrived looking plain.

17) Hate was contentious throughout the night, but love refused to fight.

18) As children love their mother, Christians are to love their congregation.

19) As kittens crave a petting hand, the cantankerous need a loving friend.

20) Love God and man, man and God.

Dear Lord, may I always love my brother as much as you love me. Amen.

CHAPTER 42

COMMANDMENTS ARE NOT AN OPTION

> Everyone who believes that Jesus is the Christ is born of God, and everyone who loves the Father loves his child as well. This is how we know that we love the children of God: by loving God and carrying out His commands. This is love for God: to obey His commands. And His commands are not burdensome. **1 John 5:1–3 NIV**

1) Godly obedience annihilates regret.
2) God's Word is armed with woe-seeking missiles.
3) God's directions never mislead.
4) In desperation, she called to the spirits of the night and entered into a world of cruel manipulation.
5) He believed in Jesus a little, and lost a whole lot.
6) As she lamented yesterday's worry, she placed God's strength back into His hands.
7) When you love the Lord with all you are, who you were, dies.
8) When God's love touches the simple, the simple become wise.
9) Those without God's love are without God.

10) Christian love reaches down and lifts others up.

11) Inconsistent prayer warriors are weak warriors at best.

12) God gave us the map of His Word and sent His Spirit to guide us.

13) God's love doesn't force us away, but His commandments snuggle us close.

14) Hate loves firefights; but Love adores peace.

15) The strong keep His commandments, but the weak let them go.

16) The dedicated read Ten Commandments, but the undecided read ten suggestions.

17) We are to love like children; but not to fight like siblings.

18) All who reject Christ eject hope.

19) Christless gods are man-made.

20) A Christless love is less love than God has for you.

21) Be not a love not.

22) The teaching is to the teacher as skin is to bones.

23) Love that reaches out of a church must also reach within.

24) Like a soothing lotion over dry skin is God's love for us.

25) She who willingly does God's will willfully follows His Word.

26) When God's children don't get along, the song they sing is flat.

27) Why do God's children fight each other? Why do they snap like turtles and growl like angry dogs?

28) Those who look out for themselves fall down on their own.

29) These things I have yet to encounter: A tree that walks, a carrot that dances, and Godly love that sows discord.

30) More protective than a subterranean bunker are the commandments of our King.

31) As a man cries over the loss of his son, God weeps over the wayward soul.

32) As a woman weeping at her mother's grave, God's commandments cry to be heard.

33) Like a puppy pouncing upon a bouncing ball, righteousness is drawn to the obedient.

34) With the toss of one commandment, they dumped the whole lot.

35) Half-baked recipes for a godly life make the critic's pen giddy.

36) Christ's followers follow the Word, not the world.

37) God's love has high standards, so hold His standard high.

38) Half faith in a whole Jesus is all bad.

Dear Lord, increase my faith that I may love you more. Amen.

CHAPTER 43

THE OVERCOMERS

> For everyone born of God overcomes the world. This is the victory that has overcome the world, even our faith. Who is it that overcomes the world? Only he who believes that Jesus is the Son of God. **1 John 5:4–5 NIV**

1) Enduring faith claims the victory of His story.
2) Faith is the first step to many miracles.
3) The cross heals the wounded.
4) Put faith ahead of victory and be victorious all your days.
5) Look up and grow up.
6) All who come over to God are overcomers in Christ.
7) It is better to overcome than to be overcome; and it is better to limp to the finish line, than to faint from a short sprint in a long race.
8) Steady faith stands over the world, but wavering faith is soon crushed by its own weight.
9) The believer lost the battle, but the skeptic lost the war.
10) Believers achieve, but doubters lose out.

11) Doubt kicked a prayer down a hill, but faith rolled it back up again.

12) Faith lifts the fallen.

13) Don't let faith be a part-time employee in your full-time world.

14) Faith is God's gift that doubt can never unwrap.

15) The Cross-road is a one-way street to God.

16) When winning is the only aim, losing is the greatest shame.

17) Riddle me this: Can one walk away from Jesus while it's day, then expect His help after dark?

18) Three things cause me wonder, even four bring marvel to my eyes: The longevity of turtles; the flight of the bumblebee; the loyalty of dogs; and the short memories of believers.

19) Dare to walk in the shadow of giants; enter the marathon of faith.

20) Conquering faith conquers all.

21) The wages of a working faith are worthless to the worrying soul.

22) When faith is first, victory is vast; when victory is first, faith is last.

23) When belief is its own creator, faith is a fantasy that teases and taunts; but when faith is a gift from God, belief breathes fire into an ice-cold heart.

24) Conquering faith is a faith never conquered.

Dear Lord, increase my faith, decrease my doubt, and open me up to miracles. Amen.

CHAPTER 44

THREE WITNESSES

> This is the one who came by water and blood; Jesus Christ. He did not come by water only, but by water and blood. And it is the Spirit who testifies, because the Spirit is the truth. For there are three that testify: the Spirit, the water and the blood; and the three are in agreement. **1 John 5:6–8 NIV**

1) God performs what His prophets foretold.
2) Abandon yourself to the man Jesus.
3) Both rabbits and lies run from the gun.
4) The wonders God has expressed through Christ are wonderful to those caressed by His love.
5) Jesus died between two thieves, but He arose alone.
6) Christ blesses us, but we distress Him.
7) Like a dove descending from heaven, God's Spirit fluttered softly, and then anointed His son.
8) False beliefs make false people.
9) Jesus-power is God-power.
10) Jesus, the God-man, can ban all sin.
11) If Jesus hadn't died, then we couldn't live.
12) God's Spirit is truth; trust the truth.

13) When witnesses chatter, their testimony doesn't matter.

14) When Christ is Lord, we are not bored.

15) Three things amaze me, even four are a maze to my mind: An infant at birth; the ways of the wind; the beauty of the butterfly; and that Jesus became flesh and dwelt among us.

16) To live is Christ; to deny is pain.

17) Jesus' baptism confirmed His identity; His death confirmed His humanity.

18) It is better to die young than to be old without God.

19) Healthy folks without God are terminally ill.

20) The Son of God is God the son.

21) Pentecost didn't cost a penny, but it makes millions rich.

Dear Lord, may I trust your Spirit more and my logic less. Amen.

CHAPTER 45

BELIEVE IT OR NOT

> We accept man's testimony, but God's testimony is greater because it is the testimony of God, which He has given about his Son. Anyone who believes in the Son of God has this testimony in his heart. Anyone who does not believe God has made him out to be a liar, because he has not believed the testimony God has given about His Son. **1 John 5:9–10 NIV**

1) God identified Jesus at the Jordan.
2) Jesus is a blood donor for you.
3) God's testimony is a Christian's truth.
4) Wild wolves and angry agnostics are howlers at heart.
5) God chose His words carefully, and the wise choose them prayerfully.
6) God knows what He is talking about and He's talking about Jesus.
7) Cynics seek choices but get chaos.
8) The wise testify for God before the world, but fools testify before they think.
9) Man seeks proofs, but God seeks us.
10) Jesus pleases God, but people aren't so easy.

11) God introduced them to Jesus, but they promptly forgot His name.

12) God stands by His Son, but few understand why.

13) God's truth is our truth, but our truth is rarely His.

14) The cross doesn't always have united appeal, but it can become the united way.

15) If you want a part in God's play, don't expect to rewrite your lines.

16) The world wants Christ's identity to be their choice.

17) Christ is a given, because God is a giver.

18) It is better to bite off your tongue than to say Jesus is one among many.

19) When fools call God a liar, the wise give them space.

20) God's opinion of Jesus is my opinion of God.

21) It is not good to tell God that Jesus was a fraud.

22) God's evidence is greater than men's proofs.

23) Granite-like faith doesn't take Christ for granted.

24) The fool dares to argue with God, but the Almighty doesn't argue with fools.

25) Accept God's witness, and witness for Christ.

26) The doubter asked nothing of God, and nothing is what she got.

Dear Lord, forgive me for doubting you, and may I always remember who God says you are. Amen.

CHAPTER 46

GOD'S SAY SO

> And this is the testimony: God has given us eternal life, and this life is in his Son. He who has the Son has life; he who does not have the Son of God does not have life. **1 John 5:11–12 NIV**

1) The Messiah saves us from ourselves.
2) Real life is just one Jesus away.
3) No one will enter heaven with a forged ticket.
4) Crisis faith is a roller coaster ride of steep dips, turns, and valleys; but "Christ-ness" faith is a steady hike up the holy hill.
5) Believing in God is a step in the right direction, but that first step requires less commitment than the ones that follow.
6) I thought I was resting in Jesus but was merely napping close by.
7) It is better to live a Spartan Christian life than to die on a bed of gold in the absence of God.
8) Godly faith and lifelong persistence avoids the void of a lifeless existence.
9) When acquitted in a trial of faith, demand an immediate retrial.
10) All who try to think themselves into heaven are numb to the truth.

11) It is better to be proven a lowly Christian than a mighty coward.

12) How are our bodies born except through our mother? How are our spirits reborn except through Christ Jesus?

13) The still small voice of Christ isn't always still and is never small.

14) When Christ is in us, He does not slumber.

15) When we have Jesus, God has us.

16) Those who stand outside of Christ will always be without joy.

17) You have heard it said that to stand for nothing is to fall for anything; but many neither stand nor fall. They sneak through life, forever in a slouch of uncertainty.

18) They who float though life like shy fireflies are afraid their light will attract the wrong kind of attention.

19) When your life is being examined in God's courts, how many character witnesses will you have?

20) Counterfeit Christianity greets Christ Jesus only when the politics are right.

21) God wants "Christ-ness" faith, not crisis faith.

22) Christ stands out in those whom He is in.

23) Those who don't have Jesus are being had.

24) In Him is life, and life in Him is good.

Good Morning, Jesus. Thank you for being there for me. It's so great to know you are always there. I pray that I will always be there too. Amen.

CHAPTER 47

THESE THINGS

> I write these things to you who believe in the name of the Son of God so that you may know that you have eternal life. **1 John 5:13 NIV**

1) A working faith in Christ has eternal benefits.
2) Eternity without Christ is one hell of a thought.
3) Jesus' gift certificates are valid for life.
4) Doubt weakens faith, and weak faith destroys commitment.
5) Believers believe, and doubters doubt, but God's promises neither fail nor fall.
6) The fool ignores the Savior, but the righteous share Him with their world.
7) Naming names may be a game, but all names are not the same.
8) Believing in names is not a game; people and names are the same.
9) As buttermilk biscuits sop gravy, believers soak up the Words of Life.
10) Just as a blade of grass can crack concrete, ignored doubt slowly fractures solid faith.
11) Jesus is the name; salvation is the game.

12) Keep Jesus in sight; stay on the right path.

13) Unanswered questions can lead to a questionable life.

14) Believe in the Christ who believes in you.

15) Let His harmony be your testimony.

16) Today's faith is tomorrow's hope.

17) Christians don't know everything, but they do know Christ.

18) As sure as thimbles need needles and needles need thimbles, answers need questions and questions need answers.

19) Dump the guesses and hope; for hope is God's guest of honor.

Dear Lord, I know that I have eternal life. Help me to live that knowledge with confidence. Amen.

CHAPTER 48

A NEW WILL AND TESTAMENT

> This is the assurance we have in approaching God: that if we ask anything according to His will, he hears us. And if we know that He hears us—whatever we ask—we know that we have what we asked of Him. **1 John 5:14–15 NIV**

1) Mature Christians pray with child-like faith.
2) True prayer is more than a want list.
3) Righteousness does it right.
4) Uncertainty sabotages prayers.
5) The righteous are confessed up and cleaned up before they are prayed up.
6) The logician and the magician easily explain away prayer.
7) Fools place their confidence in prayer, but the wise place their faith in God.
8) Desire His desires; want what God wants.
9) Anxiousness rushes God, but confidence waits upon the Lord.
10) The confused pray like children talking to Santa, but the wise ask what God wants.
11) The righteous want their life to match His blueprints, but the self-righteous want God to force His will to fit theirs.

12) Skeptics wonder *if* their prayers will be answered, but the faithful wonder *how* God will answer.

13) The desperate plead for God to change His mind, but the dedicated pray for God to change theirs.

14) The self-directed want good plans, but the godly crave only His.

15) The selfish ask God to grant their will, but the selfless ask to be a part of His.

16) The haughty make demands of God, but the humble desire to pray like Jesus.

17) The deluded dream, but the dedicated depend upon God.

18) Babies neither bring their own broom nor clean their own room; but they are cared for by those who love them.

19) The religious have faith in prayer; but for the righteous, prayer is only a tool.

20) Simple faith; effective prayer.

21) Before one can pray according to His will, she must be in sync with it.

22) Like a camel searching for water, the humble thirst for righteousness.

23) Whom does the Almighty hear? He who does not hoard sin, she who tarries not in seeking God's will, each who desires purity over pleasure, and all who crave to be set apart for God in Jesus' name.

24) Childlike faith sweeps many floors and mends many doors.

25) As geese know when and how to fly north and south, God shows the faithful which direction to fly.

26) When will He answer? When your will is His will.

27) When faith talks, God listens.

28) When confidence clears its throat, it is ready to pray.

29) A listening Lord; a praying person; an answered prayer.

Dear Lord, I am timid in Your presence because I know my shortcomings, that my personal time exceeds my prayer time. I pray that I will love You more so that I will want to be with You more. Amen.

CHAPTER 49

INTERCEDE AND PLEAD

> If anyone sees his brother commit a sin that does not lead to death, he should pray and God will give him life. I refer to those whose sin does not lead to death. There is a sin that leads to death. I am not saying that he should pray about that. All wrongdoing is sin, and there is sin that does not lead to death. **1 John 5:16–17 NIV**

1) Half a prayer on behalf of others makes us half the person we should be.
2) As boiling water scalds the skin, prayers cause boils on the devil's hide.
3) Intercession and confession pack power into the prayer.
4) Those who intercede and plead help others succeed.
5) We've seen our sister's keeper, and she is us.
6) Sin separates, but forgiveness unites.
7) Sin slips a noose around the neck, but prayer snips the strands.
8) Sin builds a wall between us and God, but forgiveness melts it to the ground.
9) Though the sinner puts money in the purse, bankruptcy of the soul awaits.

10) Critics condemn both sin and sinner, but the righteous condemn only the sin.

11) The righteous know where to find forgiveness, but the cynic declares the pathway too smooth.

12) Some laws of man extinguish life, but the laws of God grant life everlasting.

13) Like a jet leaving the runway, some abruptly separate themselves from God; but others slowly slide away like a snake slithering through grass.

14) Those who stay close to God can pray for those who don't, but the wayward praying for the wayward is like talking into a disconnected phone.

15) Though one sin may fly under the radar, its friends aren't so easy to hide.

16) Criticism eats at the spirit like termites gnawing on wood.

17) As the spider's web entangles the fly, gossip entangles the innocent.

18) Crimes against children will never be sniffed at, but fellow Christians without prayer go unnoticed.

19) It is good to pray for the forgiveness of others.

20) Better is prayer for the hurtful than vengeance.

21) Prayer is the foundation of all counseling.

22) Prayer builds; gossip destroys.

23) Forgiveness flows freely from the Father.

24) Pray for the strays and the stays.

25) Though our sister may sin, she is our sister just the same.

26) Our prayerless glares at sin put tears in the Father's eyes.

27) Prayer matters.

28) Sin happens.

Dear Lord, replace my criticism with prayer, and my apathy with care. Amen.

CHAPTER 50

THE END OF SIN?

> We know that anyone born of God does not continue to sin; the one Who was born of God keeps him safe, and the evil one does not touch him. We know that we are children of God, and that the whole world is under the control of the evil one. **1 John 5:18–19 NIV**

1) Spiritual rituals don't guarantee rebirth.
2) God stops sin's clock.
3) Worldliness corrupts goodness.
4) Sin seeks us out.
5) As sure as the sun rises and sets, God's grace and power are always there.
6) To God be the glory, and may we be the ones to give it.
7) Evil's badness and God's goodness are unevenly matched.
8) The devil knows our name, and says it all day long.
9) Though its fingers claw at my soul, Jesus will break sin's grip.
10) God offers rebirth, but the devil digs our grave.
11) Evil is in the world, but Christ is in the righteous.

12) God's protective shield is yours, but only if you are His.

13) Be in the world, but don't let the world into you.

14) Like a pack of hungry dogs, sin nips at our heels.

15) Ratchet back; regroup with Jesus.

16) Power over sin comes from God, but power over God is granted to no one.

17) Both sinner and saint need a savior.

18) Obedience to God is more precious than wealth.

19) Sparks become flame when the wood is dry.

20) When at life's Cross roads, remember the cross of Christ.

21) Like termites on wood, evil is an ever-present threat.

22) Closer to God; farther from evil.

23) Who stands vulnerable before sin? Who does temptation destroy? All who refuse to enter the birth canal of grace.

24) It is better to sleep on a bed of scorpions than to ignore the presence of evil.

25) Rainmaker and lottery; chance and poverty.

26) Like pottery waiting to be broken are they who try to tame themselves.

27) Three things cause me awe; even four do bend my knees: God's grace, Christ's love, God's power, and Satan's arrogance in the face of them all.

28) Beware of the maxims that paint life as a level playing field.

29) When sin's cold nose presses against our neck, its teeth are dangerously close.

30) Sin is but a parasite that slowly collapses its host.

31) Let goodness be a virtue, not a religion.

32) As a maggot seeks rotting flesh, evil seeks us out.

33) Can the begotten of God be influenced by sin?

34) Sin's hour of power is past at last.

35) That the world is basically evil is a basic principle of the world.

Dear Lord, you have the power to deliver me from evil. I pray that you come quickly, and that I follow in trust. Amen.

CHAPTER 51

TRUE UNDERSTANDING

> We know also that the Son of God has come and has given us understanding, so that we may know Him who is true. And we are in Him who is true—even in His Son Jesus Christ. He is the true God and eternal life. **1 John 5:20 NIV**

1) Life with Christ is a truth we can live with.
2) Denying Christ is a hell of a thing to do.
3) Understanding comes one prayer at a time.
4) Sin hinders prayer.
5) A hard head cannot expand.
6) Truth threatens hard hearts and empty heads.
7) Lies against Christ are ruthless and truthless.
8) Little talks with Jesus keep one small; but constant prayer makes one tall.
9) God is among us, not was among us.
10) God doesn't need us, but we need God.
11) Fools bray their knowledge to the mall; but the righteous bow in wonder at their ignorance.
12) Christ Jesus here and now.
13) Dare to know what He knows; He knows that you are worth loving.
14) In our need for Him, we need not be ashamed.

15) Ignore scoffers who giggle at your Bible; grow in confidence and truth.

16) A wide gap between faith and trust is an easy path to a narrow mind.

17) When God waters our faith, our understanding blossoms.

18) More facets than the world's jewels are the dimensions of knowing Christ Jesus.

19) A narrow cross threw the gates of heaven wide open.

20) Life becomes ruthless and truthless without God's love.

21) God did not send His Son for His benefit.

22) Know Christ; know truth. No Christ; no truth.

23) Believers too busy to pray stay eye-to-eye with Tom Thumb.

24) A plastic Jesus on a cross has no strength, imparts no power, and shrinks faith to the size of a germ.

25) An elastic faith has toy notions, fanciful beliefs, and an understanding like morning dew.

26) Three things that never end; even four whose ladder increases their rungs: The numerical value of travel on a Mobius strip, suffering in a fallen world, and the joy of serving Christ.

27) What can we learn from the simple sunflower? It greets the sun in the morning, and follows without complaint; then it bows when the day is done.

28) To sit with Christ is to stand at the door of understanding and to walk in truth.

29) True understanding begins with a bent knee, a broken spirit, and a shattered self.

Dear Lord, I pray that I will spend enough time with you every day so that I will know you and your truth more and more. Amen.

CHAPTER 52

THE DEADLY TREE

Dear children, keep yourselves from idols. **1 John 5:21 NIV**

1) Make your life a "no idol" zone; be idol-free.
2) Small minds can worship only what they can see.
3) Adultery and idolatry are sinister sisters.
4) Stay away from "they" and "them," and keep close to Him.
5) Idols come wrapped in strange packages and costumes that make us smile.
6) Call upon the name of the Lord your God, and other spirits will bow.
7) Worry-rituals soon turn to worship, and reverence of fear becomes a way of life.
8) Godly purity increases with godly desires.
9) A visit to idols is a corruption of faith.
10) Flirting with idols leads to dates.
11) Small idols have big appetites.
12) Idol: Indiscriminant Devourers Of Loyalty.
13) Oh woe is me; I doll a tree and dress it up to be worshiped.

14) Worship Christ of the cross, not the cross of Christ.

15) Accept no understudies for God's part in your life's play.

16) As sure as flame eaters get chapped lips, unfaithful believers get hardened hearts.

17) When idols are lifted up, downfall follows.

18) I looked for God in bars and taverns; He wasn't there. I searched for God in asceticism and diets; I found Him not. I called for God over the Internet; He made no reply. But when I turned to run to Christ; He was already there.

19) Breakfast with God is good nutrition.

20) It takes more faith to worship idols than to worship God.

21) A life without idols is a good start.

22) If man made it, don't worship it.

Dear Lord, first place is what you want. You want me to have no other Gods at all. Help me keep it so. Amen.

About the Author

Dr. Monroe Gaultney teaches at New Life Theological Seminary and Central Piedmont Community College in Charlotte, North Carolina. He is the founder of Hungry Christian Ministries (Hungrychristian.com).